BRITAIN IN OLD P

CW00731583

NORTH WALSHAM
& DISTRICT

NEIL R. STOREY

Ernest Starling, 1881–1961,
pictured as butcher's boy, 1898.

The History Press

This book is dedicated to all my family,
in memory of the past for the future

River Farm, Honing, *c*. 1938. My great-grandparents, Ellen and Frederick Griffin, are
seated in front; behind them are my great-uncles, left to right, Ernie, Fred and Don.

First published 1995 by Alan Sutton Publishing Ltd
This edition 2013

The History Press
The Mill, Brimscombe Port
Stroud, Gloucestershire, GL5 2QG
www.thehistorypress.co.uk

British Library Cataloguing in Publication Data.
A catalogue record for this book is available from the British Library.

ISBN 978 0 7509 56703 0

Typesetting and origination by The History Press
Printed and bound in Great Britain by
Marston Book Services Limited, Oxfordshire

Contents

EDWARD
STOREY
CATTLE DEALER
&
BUTCHER'S SUPPLIER

WORSTEAD and NORTH WALSHAM

Harvesting near Worstead, *c.* 1926.

North Walsham Market Place, *c*. 1870.

Introduction

The town of North Walsham and its surrounding settlements are some of the oldest in Norfolk. Considering its situation it is hardly surprising. The town is built within a declivity descending northward towards the River Ant – a tributary of the River Bure which forms the town boundary and flows through the district.

The earth upon which it stands has a sand and gravel consistency; once charmingly known as a champagne district, the whole area lends itself to farming, the fields for miles around swaying with wheat, oats and barley, and Westwick and Honing renowned for their fruit farms. The landscape, ideal for livestock, was one of the country's major high-quality meat suppliers, sheep and cattle a common sight, with their drovers and boys cramming the roadways for centuries. Trading fairs for horses and lean cattle were held on the eve and day of the Ascension (Holy Thursday) in the town and larger villages.

Neolithic flint implements, iron and bronze age relics have been recovered from numerous sites in the locality. In 1826, for example, a number of Roman burial urns were found near Edingthorpe Church. Some of the most interesting discoveries from the Roman occupation, however, were discovered in the autumn of 1844. Labourers carting sand away from Stow Heath at Felmingham caused the soil to cave in, revealing the first of about twenty dark clay urns that were discovered over the following two years. Their contents were a curious collection of figurines, coins and offertory gifts, dating from about AD 254. The Romans arrived in the area, probably via the River Ant, originally the River Smale, on the banks of which they built their fortified settlement which became known as Smaleburga; the modern village of Smallburgh is on a slightly different site.

Most of this area, the town of Walsham and its surrounding villages in the Domesday Hundred of Tunstead, was at least in part manorial lands held by the Abbey of St Benet of Holm. The Hundred was bisected by a number of pilgrim routes for local religious houses such as Bromholm Priory and its Holy Rood, The Holy Rood of Crostwight, and the Benedictine monks at St Benet's Abbey itself.

After the Norman Conquest, and especially after the accession of Edward III, who was married to a Flemish princess, the immigration of Flemish weavers was encouraged. Many settled in and around Norwich, bringing prosperity to the region for 600 years through the wool trade. Such wealth was demonstrated in the number of churches built in the area on profits from the trade. No better example can be found than that of Worstead Church, erected in the village that produced the material that became a household name. The high regard in which 'worsteds' were held caused the parish to pay more tax than North Walsham in the mid-fifteenth century. The flourishing town of Worstead once spread as far as its hamlets of Bengate, Bridgegate, Brockley, Lyngate and Withergate.

As we shall see, the area has a long reputation for nonconformity. During the Civil War North Walsham became a centre for Fifth Monarchists, and in time a village could have as many as five well-supported religious groups within its boundaries sustained in turn by an ever growing population. Following the opening of the Norwich to North Walsham turnpike in 1797, the enclosure acts at the turn of the nineteenth century and the opening of the North Walsham and Dilham Canal in 1826, the area flourished. (The tonnage and lock dues were, however, very expensive, coals and other heavy stuffs still being brought by land carriage from the coast near Mundesley or Bacton.) The wealth first brought the East Norfolk Railway, eventually the Great Eastern, and the Yarmouth and North Norfolk Railway, which became the Midland and Great Northern. An old guidebook reveals that the North Walsham district was situated betwixt 'Poppyland' and 'Broadland', and extolled its virtues of gas and electrical supplies, street lighting and well-made roads. In fact: '. . . once the sewerage scheme is completed [it will be] a residential area second to none in a popular holiday county'.

Today we all take modern life for granted. The days when horses and mules were the driving force on the roads, disturbed only occasionally by the rattle and hiss of the traction engine, seem very distant now. Gone is the life on the land when ploughmen and scythe harvest men had their 'dew drink' before work, 'levenses' mid-morning, 'noonins' at lunch and 'fourses' at about 4 p.m. Often in harvest time large flagons of beer would be brought out to quench thirst; these 'whets', 'baits' or 'snaps' were accompanied by bread 'sops'. When all was safely gathered in there would be the 'horkey' or harvest frolic. Norfolk dialect words describe many other country customs, but both the dialect and the events themselves are slowly being lost. In this book we take a look at the way people in and around North Walsham lived and worked in the past. Times were hard but the bond between country people was strong, something we must all try to carry on. I remember many great local characters 'mardling' with my grandad; most are sadly no longer with us but their stories and memories live on in the text and photographs in the following pages. Here's to their memory, the times my hair was ruffled by hard-worn hands, and when they said to me: 'Keep you on a'troshin', bor!'

Neil R. Storey
1995

6

One

NORTH WALSHAM

Drinkers in the Angel Inn Club Room, c. 1965. Cheers!

Monument to commemorate the Battle of North Walsham Heath, Toff's Loke, Norwich Road, c. 1900. In 1381 Wat Tyler's Rebellion was led in Norfolk by Geoffrey Litester of Felmingham, his brother John Litester, a dyer of Worstead, being the force's 'general'. Amassing an estimated 50,000 rebels they stormed Norwich, but were eventually forced back to North Walsham Heath to do battle with Bishop Henry de Spenser of Norwich's smaller force of more highly trained troops. Much of the rebel force was slaughtered, but the remnants retreated to the town and made their final stand in the church and nearby buildings. This monument and Stump Cross, now near the waterworks, were erected to mark the site where the battle raged, and ended the local Peasants' Revolt.

The newly constructed waterworks, Norwich Road, 1955. In 1898 test pumping was carried out on this site. In 1902 well-pumping equipment and a water tank were installed, but the town was dependent on a single set of three-throw pumps until 1924. If the call came from Bertie Appleton, waterworks' foreman, to William Morris, town surveyor, that two of the three pumps were 'out', they knew they were up against it. A reserve set was eventually installed.

Norwich Road, c. 1908. Always the important 'entrance' road to the town, the final section of the Norwich to North Walsham turnpike was opened in 1797, and attempts were always made to keep it in good repair. Originally surfaced with Wymondham flints, granite and binding silt, Norwich Road was the first to be tarmacadamed in the town.

Charles Henry Simpson's workshop, Cornish & Gaymer's Millfield Works, Norwich Road, c. 1930. Working for Cornish & Gaymer for sixty-five years, Mr Simpson was their master carver, creating masterpieces such as the bishop's throne in Norwich Cathedral. Examples of his work still exist in cathedrals, churches and mansions across the country and abroad.

Cornish & Gaymer's delivery van, c. 1917. Constructed on a 30 cwt Ford chassis, the coachwork was built at the Millfield Works. This van served the company well for many years, transporting carvings and fitters all over the county. At the time of the photograph it was driven by John Roper (father of Len Roper, the local craftsman).

Open air swimming bath and pavilion, Paston School field, Girls' High School Sports Day, 1933. Constructed in 1892 along with the tennis courts, gymnasium and rifle range, these facilities met the educational and sporting needs of pupils of Paston Grammar School and the Girls' High School for many years. The schools' field was also the drill and exercise ground of the Paston Combined Cadet Force, raised by Major Pickford DSO in 1919.

Great Eastern Railway station, c. 1934. Known as North Walsham 'Main', this was the town's first station. It was completed on 20 October 1874.

North Walsham Midland and Great Northern Town station, *c.* 1910. It is packed with team members of North Walsham Football Club, clutching their leather Gladstone bags containing their precious boots, and their supporters. The team was playing away for the Hospital Charities Shield.

Competitors line up in front of the GER Railway Bridge, Norwich Road, 22 June 1911. Starters' orders are being given by Mr Walter Pallett and 'Professor' Albert Walker. This was the One Mile Walk held as part of the afternoon sports programme during the celebrations for the Coronation of King George V. There were twenty-two entrants, and the winner was Mr A.E. Fields.

Harmer & Scott's Garage, Norwich Road, 1933. Pictured when newly purchased by Stuart Harmer and Bill Scott, the business in 'the garage by the station' went from strength to strength, becoming one of the largest motor engineers and electrical agents in the area.

Walker's Garage, 5 Norwich Road, *c.* 1910. Originally a grocer, Albert Walker experimented in selling bicycles from his Market Place shop. This was a successful venture and it eventually took over his entire business, which became Walker's Garage on Yarmouth Road. The shop pictured between these premises was also occupied by Mr Walker for a short while. Here, Albert Walker is showing his varied stock of bicycles together with his children, Lucy, Harry and Cyril.

The Bull, on the corner of King's Arms Street and Grammar School Road, *c.* 1897. This had been an alehouse since the 1860s. The unfortunate landlords were often left clearing up the mess after vehicles misjudged the fork in the road and ploughed into the entrance doors. The Bull finally met its end when demolished in August 1971, after it was declared structurally unsound.

Paston Grammar School, *c.* 1922. Founded in 1606 by Sir William Paston, it educated many well-known people. These include Archbishop Tenison, who crowned Queen Anne and George I, Louis N. Parker, the dramatist, and Admiral Nelson – commemorated here with flags flying on 21 October, Trafalgar Day. Nelson certainly went a long way from when he scrumped pears and scratched his initials in a brick in a master's garden!

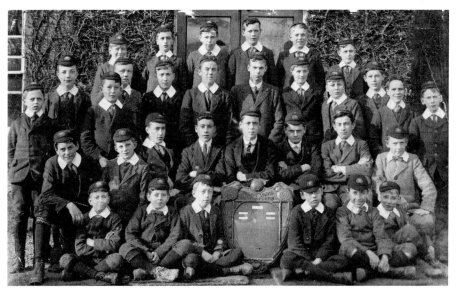

Boys of one of the Paston Grammar School houses, *c.* 1912. The houses, Tenison, Wharton (Walton at the time), Nelson and Hoste, were named after notable former scholars at the school. The house system was set up in 1911 by the headmaster, George Hare, to encourage competition.

Len Roper's workshop, Bank Loke, 1950. Apprenticed at Cornish & Gaymer, Len co-founded Foulser, Roper and Self, the well-known local builders, when Cornish & Gaymer folded. Len is seen at work on the memorial tablet bearing the names of the forty-five North Walsham men who gave their lives during the Second World War. Dedicated on 1 May 1950 by the Bishop of Thetford, the tablet, designed by Cecil Upcher of Norwich, can be seen to this day in the War Memorial chapel in St Nicholas' Church.

Founders of Wilkinson & Davies, legal practitioners, *c.* 1900. Standing on the left is Fairfax Davies, solicitor, perpetual commissioner, clerk to the Urban District Burial Board, superintendent registrar and clerk to the Guardians of the Smallburgh Union. Seated is the senior partner, John Wilkinson, solicitor, who held the above positions before Mr Davies. Standing on the right is John Dixon JP, auctioneer, estate agent, deputy superintendent registrar, future town mayor and chairman of the Urban District Council.

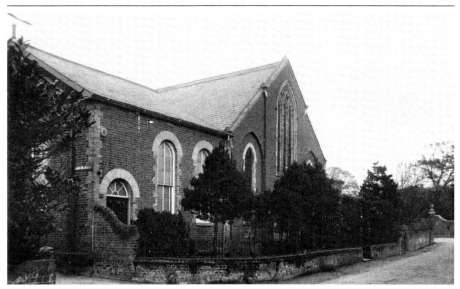

Methodist church, Grammar School Road, *c.* 1920. Methodism in the town can be traced back as far as 1797, when Richard Colls applied for a licence for a building known as a 'Methodist chapel' – probably an adapted stable or barn. A permanent building was built on Church Street in about 1820. To serve an ever-growing congregation, the present church (pictured) was built in 1890.

Women's Union meeting, held in the hall adjoining the Methodist church, Grammar School Road, 1951.

Peace Day Parade, Saturday 19 July 1919. To celebrate the Armistice and the end of the First World War there was a United Service of Thanksgiving in the Market Place followed by a grand parade, part of which is seen here on the corner of Grammar School Road.

The Limes, Yarmouth Road, c. 1920. This house was run for a number of years as a preparatory school under the Principal Miss Joanna E. Krieger. It later became an annexe to Paston Grammar School, and is now a private house.

Yarmouth Road, *c.* 1930. On the left of the picture is The Oaks Lodge, which remained standing when The Oaks, a large house that stood in its own grounds, was demolished during the 1930s. The lodge suffered a similar fate in 1960.

Police station, Yarmouth Road, *c.* 1924. When this picture was taken the station was just over ten years old. Originally the lock-up was on Vicarage Street; at the turn of the century Frederick 'Blue' Woodhouse Lovick was superintendent, and together with two constables kept order in the town.

Police parade, 1927. North Walsham and area police constables line up for inspection by Supt. Herbert Carter in front of their station and the petty sessional court house, built in 1903.

The opening ceremony at North Walsham Cottage Hospital, 27 August 1924. It was paid for by local people as a memorial to the ninety-nine local men killed during the First World War. Captain John Dixon JP gives the address before the hospital is formally opened by Her Highness Princess Marie Louise.

The start of a slow bicycle race, which was part of the Whit Monday Sports held on the People's Park, 1929. The park is now a council estate off Pound Road. The third starting marshal from the left is Ted Willey of Walker's Garage, who was eventually owner of a cycle shop in his own right. It is run today by his son Les.

Norfolk Canneries, New Road, decked out for the 1937 Coronation. The premises at Park Hall were leased by Messrs Corbett and Duncan, who began canning local produce there in 1931. By 1938 the company's turnover had risen to £43,000 per annum, enabling the purchase of Park Hall and new premises at Millfield.

The Regal Cinema, New Road, seen here in about 1977, was opened on Monday 7 September 1931 by Guy D. Fanshawe, prospective Conservative candidate for East Norfolk. The capacity audience enjoyed a programme that included British Movietone News and the main feature – Leslie Henson in *A Warm Corner*. Suffering the same fate as too many local picture houses, it closed in the late 1970s.

Floats process up New Road as part of the town's Coronation celebrations for King George VI, 12 May 1937.

Laying of the foundation stone of North Walsham ARP Casualty Service Station on New Road by Maj.-Gen. McHardy, 1940. The frisson among the Red Cross nurses to the left of the picture is caused by a spider running up one of the ladies' legs!

North Walsham has had a private bowls club for over a hundred years, with many prominent locals swelling its numbers. Club members are seen here in about 1912. Back row, left to right: -?-, Frank Marjoram, -?-, Edward Press, Edwin Simpson, Lawyer Empson. Middle row: Bob Palmer, Fred Edwards, -?-, ? Bloomfield, B. Barker, -?-, Albert Walker, ? Davison, ? Bates, Robert Chapman. Front row: Fred Marjoram, Frank Miles, Nathaniel Webster, John Dixon, ? Bacon, Leo Bircham, William Lindsey. Sitting on the ground: S. Edwards, Reg Brown, Cecil Mace.

North Walsham town firemen, 1940. They are, left to right, J.B. Craske, Fred Duglas, Ernie Emerson, George Moore, -?-, Beau Cubitt, Charlie Palmer (superintendent), W. Craske, 'Dawdler' Gee, Stanley Scott, Carl Farrow, Billy Foulser.

North Walsham cattle market, Yarmouth Road, *c.* 1947. There have been livestock and meat sales at various places in the town, from the days of the medieval flesh market in 'the Butchery' to the fair held on Ascension Eve and Ascension Day for horses and cattle. This was, however, the sale ground in living memory, when cattle were driven here by drovers and their boys for the sale.

Sid Sexton's butcher's shop, Church Plain, *c.* 1960. Your Christmas beef! From Her Majesty's estate at Sandringham, this prize beast was to grace a number of tables during that festive season. Less scrupulous butchers would acquire incredible beasts at this time of year, with up to ten customers all convinced they had a leg from the same animal!

Church Street, 1930. A policeman stands ready to direct traffic on almost the exact spot where, during the 1926 General Strike, Frederick Griffin, foreman at River Farm, Honing, saw two horses and a wagon come careering up the Market Place having broken loose. Standing his wife and small daughter in a safe place, he stood and raised his hands to the horses as they approached. Onlookers thought he would get himself killed but the horses clattered to a halt: there were few better horsemen than Fred in his day!

The post office, Church Street, *c.* 1901. At this time the postmaster was Thomas Bradshaw. His duty was to oversee the sale of stamps and registration of letters, local express messenger service and telegraphs between 7 a.m. and 8 p.m., in the days when there were nine postal collections per day and even one delivery of letters on Sundays and bank holidays!

Le Grices' grocers, Church Street, *c.* 1900. William Alexander Le Grice opened a small grocer's shop on Church Street just before the turn of the century. Business was so successful that he expanded to yet another shop in the Market Place; this was run as a general outfitters.

Hall Lane, *c.* 1950. Once known as 'Scent Bottle Alley', on account of the large open sewer that ran along its length, this road was once one of the busiest entering the town, because of all the farm traffic. It is not surprising to find that one of the oldest smithies in the town was sited here at no. 13. Run in the 1850s by Anton Dennis, its best remembered inhabitants were the Farrow family, beginning with William at the turn of the century and followed by his son Carl.

Dog Yard, 1958. So named after the Dog alehouse which once stood here and was kept by John Willimot in the mid-1830s, Dog Yard is another lost piece of North Walsham. The site was cleared to make way for Reeves' Court, flats for elderly people.

North Walsham has a very long Salvation Army tradition. Seen here is one of the earliest photographs of its first fully assembled band, in front of The Oaks during the 1890s.

Mildred Blanche Duff, born in 1860, was the daughter of Colonel James Duff, MP for North Norfolk. Her life was dedicated to helping others: attending Salvation Army meetings at the Exeter Hall in London, rising to the rank of commissioner in charge of London Slums Division in 1894 and travelling as aide-de-camp with Mrs General Bramwell Booth. She retired in 1926, and on her death in 1932 she left her home on Furze Hill to the Salvation Army. Initially a correctional centre for young boys it is now a residential home for the elderly and bears her name.

Edward Snell, the first headmaster of North Walsham Board School, 1872–1909.

Public Elementary School, Manor Road, *c.* 1887. The school was built at the expense of the school board, and cost £3,300. A fee of 1d per child per week was charged. Children provided their own stationery.

Junior School football team, 1911–12. Back row, left to right: H. Nobbs, L. Hayden, R. Atkins, B. Goulty, J. Turner, E. Amies. Front row: A. Grimes, L. Whitside, A. Mace, R. Shingles, A. Richardson. This team won the hotly contested Primary School Football Shield, beating Cromer in the final.

1/6th (Territorial) Cyclist Battalion, Norfolk Regiment, football team, 1915–16. Based in the town during the First World War, initially in the school, the battalion was moved to more permanent billets in the town but continued to use the school field for sports.

North Walsham Public Elementary School, Boys' Department choir, 1925–6. The boys' singing talents were consistently good, and they took part in the choral competitions and performances at St Andrew's Hall, Norwich, for many years.

Evacuees having dinner at North Walsham Central School, 1940. Each day 130 were served for 3d a head.

North Walsham Board School teachers, c. 1948. Back row, left to right: -?-, Clifford 'Snag' Anstice, Reggie Cubitt (headmaster), Ernest 'Chip' Bowerin, Harry Simper. Front row: Myfanwy Evans, Miss Kemshed, Mrs Bowerin, Miss Wenn.

North Walsham Central School dinner ladies, c. 1946. Under Mrs Scott (front row, second left) they worked in those austere days of rationing when almost everything was stewed – soup, lunch and tea! Prunes and lumpy custard were served for afters.

North Walsham Secondary Modern School Young Farmers Club pet show, *c*. 1951.

Children proudly show their fine rabbits at the same pet show.

Female prefects, North Walsham Secondary Modern School, 1962. Back row, left to right: Janet Sayer, Margaret Hendry, Jean Lubbock, Valerie West, Pamela Bane, June Wilkins, Jane and Sue Coleman. Front row: Christine Snowie, Janice Fisher, Linda Keeble, Diane Storey, Miss MacKenzie, Edna Puncher, Lesley Elgar, Dianne Lacey, Carol Peachment.

A young Pat Underwood walks the high beam in the school gymnasium, c. 1955. The boys look on. I remember well the feeling of dread, when George Howard the PE master (far right) would say – 'Your turn!'

High School Seniors hockey team, 1962. Back row, left to right: Cora Roberts, Miss Thrower, Edna Puncher, Helen Williamson, Susan Angell, Janet Sayer, Janice Fisher, Maureen Kirk. Front row: Christine Snowie, Carol Lowe, Diane Storey, Pamela Sandell, Josephine Nockolds, Pauline Nearney.

A clean fight please! Boys of the Junior Boxing League in the Youth Club, November 1953.

Spa Common, *c.* 1910. Spa, White Horse and Bluebell commons were enclosed between 1820 and 1830, and a number of small dwellings sprang up on them. When White Horse Common was enclosed an allotment of 35 acres was awarded as a charity to the poor; this was let for £30 a year in 1836, and the profit from it was distributed in coals.

Prize winners at the North Walsham, Aylsham and Cromer Agricultural Show, *c.* 1908. The show was once held triennially in each respective town and was a chance to show prize cattle, survey new machinery and mardle 'hew the season hev' fared'.

Bluebell Common, *c.* 1905. This view from the bottom of Marshgate shows the Bluebell Tavern, from which the common took its name; the pub existed long before the common was enclosed. One cannot help but wonder what the ales were like in 1789, when Daniel Howard was the landlord.

Frank 'The Guv'nor' Randell with his stand at an agricultural show, *c.* 1925. Randell's, which opened in 1865, produced agricultural machinery and implements from their St Nicholas Foundry Works off Bacton Road for over a hundred years.

Bacton Road, *c.* 1930. This thoroughfare was once known as Reeves Lane. For many years one of the small inclines beside the road was known as Gibbet Hill, after the macabre warning to others that was erected there in the mid-eighteenth century. It contained the body of William Suffolk, who had murdered Mary Beck during an argument over the sale of three bushels of wheat. Executed on Castle Hill, Norwich, he was returned to the town and hung in chains near the scene of the crime.

Members of North Walsham St John Ambulance Brigade in front of their newly dedicated ambulance in the Market Place, 22 August 1948. Their headquarters were and still are in Preference Place, on Bacton Road.

Back Street, 1955. Along with Cock Street and most of Vicarage Street, this is now buried under a large car park.

Empson House, c. 1904. At this time, it was the home of Charles Henry Burton, the butcher. The house still stands today at the old point junction of Back Street and Cock Street.

Cock Street, 1955. Situated here was the town's first fixed fire engine station. The town's first appliance was a Newsham fire pump, purchased in about 1725, and pulled on a dray crewed by twenty-two volunteer firemen.

Jack Hewitt, saddler and harness makers' shop, Vicarage Street, 1927. This was one of the last true full-time craftsmen's shops. With full mechanization on the farm and the advent of the motor car this fine old shop closed in 1964. Jack's assistant George Turner is pictured.

Ellis' Confectioners, 7 North Street, 1920. This shop was run by the widow of Elijah Ellis, the chimney sweep. It is pictured with the young shop assistant, fifteen-year-old Olive Simpson, in the doorway.

Vicarage Street, originally known as Church Gate, *c*. 1958. One of David Fisher's famous circuit theatres opened in the street in 1828. In 1845 the building became a National School, and at the end of the nineteenth century the Church Rooms, scene once more of local performances and entertainment.

1st North Walsham Scout Troop leaving for camp from Ship Yard, 1951. Back row, left to right: Mike Ling, Geoff Griston, Michael Gibbons, Michael Jackson, Vernon Fiske, John Patterson, -?-, Tony Fiske. Front row: Scoutmaster 'Nobby' Clarke, Cyril Morris, Bob Curtiss, ? Griffiths, Ron Fiske, Raymond Howard, Phillip MacLean, Brian Bird.

North Walsham dustbin men, 1960.
They are, left to right, Wally Appleton,
'Dickie' Bird, Cyril Griffin and Stanley
Davison.

Billy John Jay, the road sweeper,
c. 1960. Known and respected
as a good roadman, what he
couldn't sweep up he would
pick up.

Frank Mann's Carriage Builders, Vicarage Street, 1912. The site was originally George Easy's Wheelwright and Gig Makers in the 1830s. Until the 1870s it was owned by William Drake and Jeremiah Harvey respectively; then George Gee took over and expanded the business. He was joined by his son on another site in Norwich Road, and eventually sold the Vicarage Street business to Frank Mann in 1912.

George Moore's Handsewn Bootmakers, Nelson Street (now Mundesley Road), c. 1910.

Miss Grace M. Holloway, matron at the Lower House VAD Hospital, 1915–19.

The Lower House on Mundesley Road, with resident casualties in front, 1917. Along with Wellingtonia House, this was handed over to become an auxiliary war hospital during the First World War. Lower House had eleven beds, and during the war years admitted 714 patients. It was the last of many such hospitals in the county to close, on 20 March 1919.

Jack Hall's Fruiterers & Florist, 1 Nelson Street, now Mundesley Road, 1906. This is one of the fondly remembered family businesses of the town, now sadly lost. This particular shop was begun at the turn of the century by John 'Jack' Hall, and carried on and expanded by his son Freddie and wife Winnie.

George William Hedge's garage, 30–2 Mundesley Road, *c.* 1930. Founded in the early 1920s the business went from strength to strength, beginning with motor and cycle engineering and complete car overhauls, and moving on to deal in bicycles and wireless sets. It is still a garage today.

Bob Long's Boot Retailers on the corner of Cromer Road and Mundesley Road, *c.* 1912. Following in his father Francis' footsteps, Bob took the shop on the corner at the turn of the century. A lifetime follower of North Walsham Town FC, he made the boots for the whole team – and even the lace-up footballs they played with.

Cromer Road (once known as Antingham Lane), *c.* 1910. At no. 8 was the Rising Sun, one of the country's smallest pubs. On the left is the Congregationalist Chapel, built in 1857 for £1,200.

Holly House, Cromer Road, *c.* 1903. This was once home to Captain Simpson, the man responsible for the local anti-invasion forces during the Napoleonic War.

North Walsham Town FC, 1913–14 season. Formed in 1879, this is Norfolk's oldest surviving amateur football club. It was nicknamed 'The Angels' after the original clubrooms in the Angel Inn; the pitch was close by, up Aylsham Road.

North Walsham Hornets FC, 1924 Charity Shield winners. Back row, left to right: Len Roper, ? Brown, 'Tubby' Cutting, ? Hart, Jack Sydell, Cliffy Whiteside, 'Daddy' Hart. Front row: Bob Long, David Roe, Bob Hendry, Mick Gold (captain), Pat Totten, Joe Bush, 'Tiddler' Hart.

North Walsham Wednesdays FC, 1928. This team comprised players who, because of work commitments, could not normally play on Saturdays but only on the town's early closing day – Wednesday.

North Walsham Veterans FC, 1929. The team is pictured in front of the Paston School field pavilion.

North Walsham Steam Laundry staff, Cromer Road, c. 1901. The laundry was founded in 1900, with Mr and Mrs J.A. Ogilvy as managers, and was known as 'The High Class Family Laundry'. Even after a devastating fire in 1906 the business went from strength to strength. Laundry was collected over a 20 mile radius. Before the First World War sheets were laundered with a specially requested starch when the Kaiser stayed at the Hotel de Paris in Cromer!

North Walsham Girl Guides, c. 1928.

The Elms Boarding and Day School for Girls, North Street, *c.* 1905. Founded in 1877 on Mundesley Road by Misses Maria and Jane Cooke, the school rapidly expanded to these new premises at The Lawns. They provided '. . . a thorough training for girls, careful attention being paid to their moral training and physical comfort'.

In 1922 The Elms became The Girls' High School; Miss K. Worsnop MA was the principal. Seen here on the lawn are sixth-form girls in about 1933.

1st North Walsham Company Boys Brigade, 1905.

Norwich Co-operative Society, 1921. In this year it was newly re-opened as the original building had been burnt down while commandeered by the military in 1916. Many can still remember the dances held in the clubroom above the store.

Market Street, *c.* 1925. This was once known as Angel Street after the ancient Angel Inn situated there. It was down this unfortunate street that practically all the liquid sewage of the town flowed, along brick gutters (many of the bricks badly worn so that sewage often soaked into the ground) and through an old barrel drain under Fayer's Bakehouse to the town drain on Catchpit Lane, and on to the canal.

Interior of Rackstraws quality grocers, 16 Market Street, *c.* 1950. The shop was opened in 1925 by Percy Rackstraw, who built up an enviable reputation for fine foods. People always remember the fine array of cooked meats and the variety of smells from the tins of coffee, tea, cheeses and preserves.

Star Supply Stores, 10 Market Street, 1908. The special Christmas offer on display is a half pound of 1*s* 6*d* tea given free to every customer spending 2*s* 6*d* or over.

Looking down Market Street, at 6.30 a.m. on the morning of Tuesday 21 June 1897; the bunting is up and ready for the celebrations later that day in honour of Queen Victoria's Diamond Jubilee.

Cubitt's Grocers, originally known as The Stores, Jubilee House, 21–2 Market Place, *c.* 1904. Charles Cubitt began in the 1850s as a grocer and draper, expanding quickly to wholesale and retail linen and woollen draper, grocer, tea dealer and funeral furnisher! In 1887, in honour of Queen Victoria's Jubilee, the building was named Jubilee House.

Cubitt's Grocers, 6 King's Arms Street, *c.* 1930. In the 1870s Charles Cubitt's son joined the business, and an additional store was opened on King's Arms Street; this specialized in cooked meats, game and tinned foods.

King's Arms Street, *c.* 1910. The town hall was on the site of today's Jobcentre. On 27 August 1899 it was discovered on fire. The local fire appliance arrived but no water could be found for its hoses. Robert Walpole Palmer, owner of the King's Arms, sent one of his riders, Jockey Elvin, round to the local farms to get water carts. Within half an hour thirty of them were supplying the pumps, but sadly the building was lost.

Phitwell House, King's Arms Street, *c.* 1902. Situated next to the old town hall, Edward Rayne was a ladies' and gentlemen's bespoke tailor and outfitter.

North Walsham Detachment Norfolk Army Cadet Force, 1940.

Children singing the National Anthem enter the Market Place on 21 June 1897 to start the day's celebrations that marked Queen Victoria's Diamond Jubilee. Over 2,000 people attended the celebrations and dinner in the Market Place. The children were each presented with a medal and four tickets: the first for fruit, nuts and an orange, the second for ginger beer, the third for a bun and patty, and the fourth for a toy. These were all presented in the afternoon on the recreation ground.

The Coronation bullock presented by Sewell and Pages' butchers, exhibited in the Market Place on 15 June 1911. As part of the Coronation celebrations for George V, a competition to guess the bullock's weight was held. The correct weight was 71 stone 9 lb, and the winner of the first prize cup (presented by Frank Miles the watchmaker) was George Mace. The 260 tickets that were sold raised £13.

Some of the 3,100 diners tuck into the Coronation celebration dinner in the Market Place, 22 June 1911. They polished off 213 stone of beef, £6 2s 8d worth of pickles, 100 stone of bread, 78 stone of pudding, 144 gallons of beer and 7½ barrels of ginger beer!

The opening of the drinking fountain in front of the Market Cross, 20 June 1912. It was erected as a permanent memorial to the Coronation of King George V and Queen Mary. The commemorative service was led by the Revd Aubrey Aitken, and in the foreground of this picture are the schoolchildren who sang 'God Save the King', 'Here's a Health unto His Majesty' and 'Three Cheers for the Red, White and Blue!'

North Walsham Market Cross, *c.* 1900. This ancient focal point of the town was built in the mid-sixteenth century by Thomas Thirlby, Bishop of Norwich, and replaced an earlier structure on the site. The cross was almost completely destroyed by the town fire of 1600, but Bishop Redman had it rebuilt in 1602. Passing into the hands of the Ecclesiastical Commissioners in 1830, it was later sold to the town, and was completely restored at a cost of nearly £200 in 1899. At this time a clock and bell were also installed, by John Juler the local watchmaker.

William Bullimore's drapers, Norfolk House, 20 Market Place, *c.* 1890. This was one of the first shops in the town to have gas installed, but it was not until 1926 that a telephone was installed; connection to the town sewage system followed even later. After Mr Bullimore, the shop was occupied for many years by George Burton ('G.B.') Fuller, draper and founder of the local St John Ambulance Division in 1924. The first meetings were held in the back room of this shop.

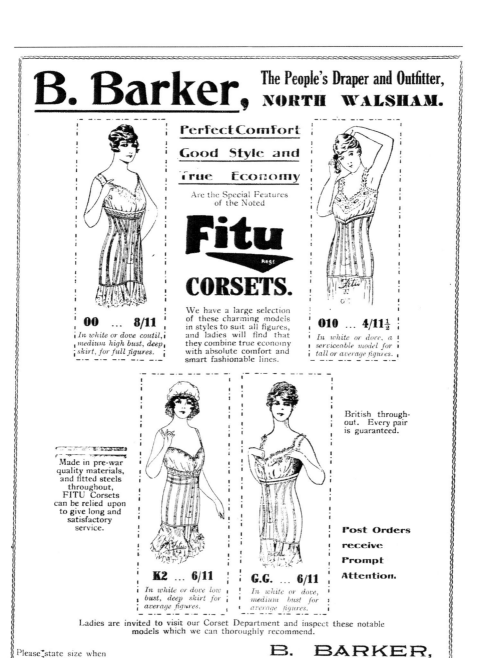

B. Barker,

The People's Draper and Outfitter, NORTH WALSHAM.

Perfect Comfort
Good Style and
True Economy

Are the Special Features
of the Noted

Fitu
CORSETS.

We have a large selection
of these charming models
in styles to suit all figures,
and ladies will find that
they combine true economy
with absolute comfort and
smart fashionable lines.

00 ... 8/11

*In white or dove coutil,
medium high bust, deep
skirt, for full figures.*

010 ... 4/11½

*In white or dove, a
serviceable model for
tall or average figures.*

British through-
out. Every pair
is guaranteed.

Made in pre-war
quality materials,
and fitted steels
throughout,
FITU Corsets
can be relied upon
to give long and
satisfactory
service.

Post Orders

receive

Prompt

Attention.

K2 ... 6/11

*In white or dove low
bust, deep skirt for
average figures.*

G.G. ... 6/11

*In white or dove,
medium bust for
average figures.*

Ladies are invited to visit our Corset Department and inspect these notable
models which we can thoroughly recommend.

Please state size when
ordering by post.

B. BARKER,
Waterloo House, North Walsham.

Advertising leaflet for Benjamin Barker's, the long-established drapers in Waterloo House in the Market Place, 1919. This advert was barred from appearing in the parish magazine as 'its contents are simply too vulgar for parochial publications'!

International Stores, 18 Market Place, c. 1909. Promising 'value always', the International was in various locations in the town for many years; its own brand of tea and tinned foods was especially popular.

Harry Carpenter's Fruiterers, Florist and Tea Rooms, 34 Market Place, c. 1925. This shop is well remembered at Christmas for its spread of seasonal fare, in the days when stockings were stuffed with nuts and maybe an orange!

Market Place, *c.* 1950. Many of these shops and businesses, such as London Edwards, Jeary's sweet shop, Marjoram Bros, Randells, Currys and the Cross Keys Hotel, have now gone.

What am I bid? A Market Place auction, *c.* 1902. To the top left is Frank Miles' Jewellers and Opticians, which appears in a local saying: 'North Walsham is Long at each end [Bob Long, boot maker, Mundesley Road, and Annie Long, confectioner, top of the Market Place] and Miles in the middle!'

Miss Elizabeth Harmer Hunter's Private Girls School, The Terrace, *c.* 1908. One of a number of private schools in the town at the turn of the century, this was originally a dame school, which had been set up by Miss Hindry in the 1880s.

A last look down the town, *c.* 1910. To the left can be seen some of the agricultural machinery for display and sale in front of Randells' Market Place hardware shop. On Thursday (market day) Randells were eligible for a stall toll; when the steward went round to collect he would turn a blind eye if they packed away early, but if they didn't the assistant responsible would have tuppence stopped out of his wages!

St Nicholas' Church, *c.* 1910. The imposing tower, once one of the tallest in Norfolk, has been left in its ruinous state after two falls, one in 1724, the other in 1836. The churchyard has now had its tombstones moved to the sides, and the railings went to the war effort salvage collectors.

The tomb of Sir William Paston, near the altar, *c.* 1920. The founder of Paston School arranged for his own monument to be constructed before his death. Employing John Key, a London freemason, the tomb was erected at a cost of £200. Sir William died two years after its completion in October 1610.

St Nicholas' church choir, 1903. In the middle of the back row is John Dixon JP, the church organist and choirmaster for many years. To the right may just be seen the box for the tower restoration fund!

St Nicholas' church choir, ready to move off to sing at the opening of the War Memorial Cottage Hospital, 1924. Back row, left to right: Ernie Gee, Harold Amiss, 'Monkey' Coleman, the Revd Harry Harcourt Thorns, John Dixon (choirmaster and organist), George Robinson. Middle row: John Mace, Billy Hewitt, Frank Osbourne, Billy Wright, Herbert Booth, Stanley Raynor, Fred Brown, Reggie Suffling. Front row: Arthur Oliver, Frank Craigie, Claude Riches, Sidney Thirtle, Teddy Flaxman, Leslie Edwards, Oliver Cousins, Ray Coleby.

Two

WESTWICK, SWANTON ABBOT, SCOTTOW, BUXTON AND LAMMAS

Jimmy Davison, 'King of the Mole Catchers', netting sparrows probably for sparrow pie, Swanton Abbot, c. 1925.

Westwick Hall, *c.* 1910. This is one of the most delightful seats in the county; it was built in about 1710 by John Berney, Esq., and the estate comprises 1,500 acres. Berney also had made a 5 mile carriage drive set in a 500 acre plantation, for which he received a medal from the Society of Arts.

St Botolph's Church, Westwick, *c.* 1910. Set in the park of Westwick House this dates from the fifteenth century and contains monuments to the incumbents of the hall, the Berneys and Petres.

Westwick Arch, *c*. 1925. Built in about 1780, the arch marked the entrance to the estate and was also a very grand dovecote. After the diversion of the Norwich to North Walsham turnpike, the arch straddled the road, and a lodge was erected on each side. The arch was demolished in September 1981 in the face of much public outcry.

The post office kept in one of the lodges, and its sub-postmaster William 'Tuffun' Watling, who also dealt in sweets and groceries, are well remembered, although this story goes back to the early 1920s. Because of repeated thieving of sweets by local boys 'Tuffun' kept a loaded shotgun in the corner. One cheeky young lad, Percy Steward, went in one afternoon and said 'Good afternoon Mr Tuffun!' Obviously having had enough that day Mr Watling grabbed his shotgun; it went off, blasting the ceiling and showering plaster all over the shop. Percy and the other boys left quickly!

Obelisk or gazebo, Westwick Park, c. 1930. Standing 90 ft high, the observation tower was built over 200 years ago by John Berney. Local legend tells that it was constructed to enable his daughter Elizabeth to keep an eye on her married sister, Julia Brograve, who lived at Worstead House. The iron observation gallery was blown down in 1970.

Camp of the 1st Royal Devon Yeomanry on Westwick Park, 1915. When the full mobilization for war began every stretch of suitable field and parkland was drawn into military use, for the marshalling of troops and as a base to acquire mounts for military service.

Painters line up for the photographer, a welcome break from redecorating Westwick Hall, c. 1910.

The once-familiar and beautiful sight of the cherry orchards on the Westwick Estate, c. 1930. Locals would band together with their children to harvest the delicious crop.

Cottage and roadway through Westwick Woods, *c.* 1905. This was a very popular place in Victorian and Edwardian times for family afternoon constitutionals, and iron benches circling the trees were installed after the railings alongside Captain's Pond became regularly too crowded.

The road by Captain's Pond, Westwick, *c.* 1908. The pond is thought to be named after Captain William Varlo who married the lord of the manor's daughter, probably in the eighteenth century. Once part of the bustling Norwich to North Walsham turnpike, it was here in the nineteenth century that William Cooper, the famous North Walsham coachman, overturned his coach and was killed.

Skaters on Captain's Pond, Westwick, 1938/9. It was a bitterly cold winter, and the surrounding area suffered floods when the snow and ice thawed.

St Michael's Church, Swanton Abbot, *c.* 1920. The present church dates from about 1350. The foundations, however, date back to when the village name was spelt Swaneton – meaning the 'tun' or settlement of the swineherds. In 1044 Edward the Confessor confirmed that the church was given to St Benet's Abbey; subsequently the village became known as Swanton Abbot to distinguish it from all other Swantons.

Swanton Abbot Wesleyan chapel and post office, *c.* 1910. This was certainly a nonconformist village at the turn of the century, when there were Wesleyan, Wesleyan Reform and Swedenborgian chapels. The post office was run by several generations of the Howard family, starting at the turn of the century with Edward Howard.

Swanton Abbot Gala, *c.* 1925. Two young men compete on the sticky pole, much to the amusement of the onlookers.

Swanton Abbot and Westwick FC, winner of the St Faith's League Championship 1930–1 season.

Scottow church, *c.* 1910. The church is built in a mix of Early English and Perpendicular styles; the parish register dates from 1558. There are strong connections with the Durrant family of Scottow Hall: the organ was presented by Sir H.T.E. Durrant Bt in 1844, and there are numerous monuments to members of the family, including an obelisk to Davey Durrant Bt, who died in 1757, constructed by the notable ecclesiastical carver George Storey of Norwich.

Scottow Hall, *c.* 1904. This fine eighteenth-century hall was the seat of Sir Thomas Durrant Bt in 1797.

Three Horse Shoes public house, Scottow. Known to locals as the 'Scutta Hu'shooes', it is pictured in about 1910 when it was kept by William James Tooke, first in a long line of that family to keep the pub. Especially remembered are Alan Tooke and his mother Amelia during the 1930s and '40s.

The Pank family in front of the Oddfellows Hall, *c.* 1910. The hall was erected beside the pub in 1844 by Sir Henry J. Durrant Bt, originally for meetings of the Durrant Lodge of Oddfellows, Manchester Unity. The head of the Pank family, Bob, owned the house on the turning off the Norwich Road on the North Walsham side of Scottow; thus explaining its name of Pank's Corner.

The Fairstead, just off the Norwich Road, Scottow, *c.* 1905. To the right of the picture behind the postman is the post office, kept at this time by Alfred Bird. Mail arrived by cart from Norwich at 5.20 a.m. and 5 p.m.

St Andrew's Church, Buxton, *c.* 1908. Built during the thirteenth century, St Andrew's was thatched until the early nineteenth century when it was visited by the Revd Francis Blomefield, the historian. Sadly falling into decay, the church was almost entirely rebuilt in 1881. To the left of the picture is the National (Infants) School, erected in 1855 for sixty children.

William Digby, the sexton, with his wife Sarah and their children Bertie and Kathleen at their cottage in Buxton, 1907. Sarah, who had lived in the village all her life, went on to become one of Buxton's oldest inhabitants, surviving to see her 103rd birthday.

Buxton church choir, Harvest Festival, 1903. Standing, left to right: W. Watts, P. Woodhouse, C. Woods, W. Digby, A. Cushion, G. Copland, P. Watts, R. Lane, W. Lubbock, H. Gould. Seated: P. Child, G. Lane, Miss Babington, E. Lubbock, the Revd Alured Elliot Black MA, F. Frosdick, E. Gould. Seated on the ground: B. Abbs, P. Arterton.

Funeral cortège for 792 Cpl. Charles James Povey 2nd/1st Battery (Berkshire) Royal Horse Artillery. He died aged forty-seven while his unit was stationed in and around Buxton on 16 April 1915.

This wintry country scene shows Coltishall Road, Buxton, just after the turn of the century. It is not hard to imagine the locals, hit by poverty, trudging up this road to the local house of industry, or workhouse, which stood there.

Buxton Mill, *c.* 1900. The mill was built in 1754 on the River Bure for milling flour and it worked well into this century. In the 1930s the miller was William Charles Duffield. The Buxton Roller Mills also operated as coal, corn, cake, seed and salt merchants. Even after a number of fires in its lifetime the mill still stands today, now business premises and a restaurant.

This animated scene shows Mill Street, Buxton, *c.* 1905. This was the main street of Buxton. Many people will surely remember Sid Ayden, the village storekeeper, and Jack Larwood, the hairdresser, from the 1920s and '30s.

Lion Corner, Buxton, *c.* 1905. The corner was named after the ancient Black Lion pub on the corner, kept for a number of years by Beno Claude Woodhouse. The pub was always an important meeting place for locals. Even the earliest minutes of a vestry meeting, from 1833, record: 'Resolved the meeting to adjourn to the Lion public house to consider the accounts'!

Brook Street, *c.* 1900. This fine scene had changed little from the time of Thomas Cubitt, a journeyman carpenter born in Buxton in 1788. His great success grew when he went to London, eventually becoming responsible for building half of old Bloomsbury and much of Belgravia.

The Red House Industrial School, Buxton, *c.* 1909. It was founded by John Wright as an 'establishment for the religious and industrial training of forty offenders under the age of 20' in 1852. After the 1908 Parliamentary Act the building was turned into a Borstal. By 1926, however, the reformatory's purpose changed again, and 'not quite normal' children weeded from Home Office schools were educated here. Today we have a better understanding of how to treat young people who have a 'bad start' in life; the good work carries on with the Small School at Red House.

St Andrew's Church, Lammas, *c.* 1910. Built during the reign of Henry I beside the River Bure, it fell into disrepair until 1887 – when it was restored at a cost of £1,200 under the direction of Mr H.J. Green, a Norwich architect.

Old Manor House, Lammas, *c.* 1900. At this time it was home to Phillip Harbord JP, well-known local landowner. Farming plays a key role in any rural community, and this village probably derives its name from the Anglo-Saxon for Lamb's fen or marsh. Lammas lands, that is land on which tenants were bound to pay their rents on Lammas Day – 1 August – may also be connected in some way, although Lammas had its name long before any such obligation existed.

Lammas Road, *c.* 1905. Just off this road is the old Quaker burial ground. Here lie a mother and daughter acclaimed for their books – Mary and Anna Sewell; the latter is the author of Black Beauty, published in 1877, the year before she died.

The weir pool beside the Anchor of Hope pub, Lammas, c. 1910. On this idyllic summer's day, as a family fish the quiet waters, nobody could have imagined the effects of the deluge of rain here in August 1912.

The weir pool burst its banks and Lammas was extensively flooded on 26 August 1912. It had been a wet season, the rainfall totalling 11.27 inches during the month, but over the night of 25/6 August about 7 inches of rainfall caused the county's greatest flood, over thousands of acres, and with damages exceeding £200,000.

Three

GUNTON, ANTINGHAM, FELMINGHAM, SWAFIELD, EDINGTHORPE, WITTON, CROSTWIGHT AND HONING

Frederick Griffin, River Farm foreman, with his team of Suffolk Punch horses, with his son Ernest riding trace horse on 'The Roundabouts' field. They are harvesting with the binder at Honing in about 1930.

Sir Charles Harbord, 5th Baron Suffield, PC, GCVO, KCB, DL, JP. Born in 1830, he inherited the Gunton Estate from his half-brother at the age of twenty-three. A fine sportsman in every field he was the subject of the couplet: 'A rider unequalled – a sportsman complete/ A rum 'un to follow, a bad 'un to beat'. A courtier of high standing and confidant of King Edward VII, he never neglected his estate or locality, investing in many local industries and sports. He was also a generous president of the Norfolk and Norwich Music Festival. It was a sad loss for the county when he died in the spring of 1914.

Gunton Hall, *c.* 1910. From Stuart times this was the seat of the Harbord family (Lord Suffield). Sir William Harbord, who inherited the estate in 1742, commissioned Matthew Brettingham to build the hall; it was enlarged by James Wyatt in 1785. The older part of the hall, including the library, was gutted by fire on Monday 18 December 1882.

Tower Lodge, *c.* 1920. This lofty Regency lookout still straddles the drive, and has a commanding view of the estate and plantations of 1,000 acres, portions of which are in Suffield, Thorpe Market and Hanworth.

St Andrew's Church, Gunton, *c.* 1920. This magnificent building was erected at the expense of Sir William Harbord KB in 1769, and was designed by Robert Adam at the same date. It stands on the site of the earlier church.

Apprentice milliners and dressmakers of Miss Sarah Suffling's School on Hanworth Common, *c.* 1910.

Antingham churches, *c.* 1905. Local legend tells that the two churches standing so close to each other were built by two sisters – Mary and Margaret. St Mary's, built by the virtuous sister, remains, but St Margaret's, built by the dissolute sister, has fallen into ruin; only its ivy-clad tower remains.

Antingham Bone Mill, *c.* 1920. This mill, built at the turn of the nineteenth century, was situated in the basin of the North Walsham and Dilham Canal and at the source of the River Ant. It operated from the turn of the century under Edward Darby Horsfield, farmer, bone crusher and artificial manure manufacturer.

St Andrew's Church, Felmingham, *c.* 1905. The church was extensively rebuilt in red brick Georgian style in 1742, but its tower is fifteenth-century. After the heavy gales of 1894–5 yet further reconstruction was required, as the roofs of the nave and tower had been destroyed and the south buttress of the tower and part of the churchyard wall had blown down.

Felmingham Rectory, *c.* 1900. Built in 1870 in the gift of the Bishop of Norwich, the rectory was inhabited in 1900 by the Revd Henry John Langley MA. In 1900 the Rectory still owned 14 acres of glebe land, and was endowed with one-fourth of the rectoral tithe.

St Nicholas' Church, Swafield, *c.* 1910. This fine late fifteenth-century church stands high above the present village. The original village was near the church, and was surrounded by an iron age defence ditch. Local folklore tells that it was moved when the lord of the manor wanted to build a new house; he didn't want to have the peasants looking down on him, so he moved the village to the bottom of the hill!

All Saints' Church, Edingthorpe, *c.* 1905. This is a fine old church with a round Norman tower, and was built in about 1400. The settlement, as its name suggests, is much older: Edingthorpe is probably derived from a mix of Old Norse and Old English, meaning Eadhelm's hamlet or secondary settlement.

Edingthorpe schoolchildren, 1914. In 1875, when the total population was 200, a school board for the united parishes of Paston and Edingthorpe was formed. The school for 100 children was erected in 1878, with Mrs Blyth as the mistress.

Royston Bridge Staithe, *c.* 1910. Known during the nineteenth century as Austin Bridge, it was built along with the Staithe in about 1825. Wherries navigating the North Walsham and Dilham Canal brought cargoes here that were destined for North Walsham and the granary store and warehouse there. The Wherry and Waterman pub was kept at the turn of the century by a number of generations of the Dixon family.

St Margaret's Church, Witton, *c.* 1920. Inside are a number of eighteenth-century monuments to the Norris family. John Norris, who began to build Witton Hall in 1770, sent Richard Porson, the village prodigy of East Ruston and future professor of Greek at Cambridge, to Eton (see page 108). He also founded the Norrisian Professorship of Divinity at Cambridge.

Witton School Group, *c.* 1925. The school for forty children was erected in 1834 by Lady Wodehouse, using an endowment of £10 left by John Norris.

Lou Pestell, a local tramp, *c.* 1920. She is remembered by many for her almost pure white eyes and crab-like walk, looking over her shoulder every few paces. One night a local policeman who was cycling down a country lane hit two sudden bumps, and ended up in a ditch. As he recovered himself, a dark swathed figure loomed above him – Lou Pestell, saying 'You've just run over my legs and woke me up!'

Dairy Farm, Witton, *c.* 1901. At this time it was the home of Bernard Cubitt.

Witton Windmill, *c.* 1910. This Norfolk post mill was at Witton Bridge; the miller for many years from the turn of the century was William Andrews.

Across the sheaves of wheat is Ebridge Mill, *c.* 1910. A mill has been here for hundreds of years: it was recorded in the Domesday Book and was known as Everbupes Watermill in Henry VIII's reign. The mill was steam- and water-driven, grinding grain and bone; for many years it has been run by the family firm of Cubitt & Walker.

Cubitt & Walker carts, *c.* 1900. The carts were driven into this small pond near the mill for a wash down after the daily deliveries.

All Saints' Church, Crostwight, *c.* 1905. The church's once fine tower is shown. In 1910 it had become so dangerous that it was removed and capped in red tile. In 1905 the population of Crostwight was seventy.

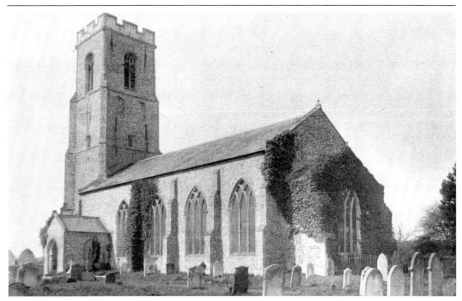

Church of St Peter and St Paul, Honing, *c.* 1910. Within are a number of interesting memorial tablets. One is to Edward George Cubitt, Esq., who served with the 4th Dragoons in the Peninsular Wars and entered Paris with the Army of Occupation in 1815, living so long afterwards that people had almost forgotten the Crimean War. An interesting parallel is recorded on a tablet to some of his descendants: the loss of three brother officers, Edward, Victor and Eustace Cubitt, during the First World War.

Honing Street, *c.* 1910. To the right of the picture is the old village hall, originally built as a temperance hall. In the 1920s its purpose changed to a men's club; it later became a parochial meeting hall, and eventually the village hall. Very recently a new village hall was built nearby.

The Stores, Honing, *c.* 1901. This shop was established in 1893. When pictured, it was in the hands of the Fletcher family – grocers, milliners and outfitters. This shop is, however, best remembered when kept by Fiske and Tench during the '20s and '30s.

Milkers at River Farm, Honing (owned by Mrs Hilda Mary Finch), *c.* 1934. Left to right: Ernest Griffin, Jimmy Strike, Oswald Griffin.

Robert Osborne, basket, bunt, sieve and wicker hurdle maker, Honing, *c.* 1912.

Honing Primitive Methodist chapel, *c.* 1905. This was built in 1883 by Edward George Cubitt JP, lord of the manor, at the grand cost of £250. The highlight of the year for many was the Sunday School outing to Bacton; the horses pulling the carts had their brasses polished, bright ribbons braided in their manes and docked tails, while the carts were also gaily ribboned with floral decorations, everybody was in their Sunday best – what a sight!

Honing West signal box, *c.* 1935. The two Honing signal boxes (Honing East box was a short way along the track on the other side of the station) were welcome additions to this busy stretch of rail when they were built in 1901. The signalmen were Mr Turner and Mr Davy, who was a staunch local Methodist.

Honing post and telegraph office, *c.* 1922. The village war trophy field gun stands outside. The sub-postmaster was Robert James Sandell, whose daughters are remembered literally running telegrams across the village with their skirts flying!

Honing Hall, *c.* 1910. Built in 1748 for the grand sum of £513, enlarged and partly 'modernised' in 1875, the hall stands in about 50 acres of parkland designed by Repton. It has been held for generations by the Cubitt family, renowned for their fruit growing industry.

Henry James Thouless (1864-1933), pictured 1924. A noted Norfolk entomologist and leading light of the Norfolk and Norwich Naturalist Society, he is remembered collecting his specimens in the Dilham area, wearing his wide-brimmed felt hat and lozenge-shaped specimen tin slung over his shoulder. Seen wading through ditches, even plucking beetles from dung, Thouless was considered 'touched' at best by locals. But his serious and methodical research about beetles and butterflies provided Norwich Castle Museum with a unique collection, which was presented after his death. He is buried in St Mary's churchyard, Wroxham, near the rich hunting grounds that he knew and loved so well.

Briggate Mill and wharf, c. 1910. Originally a fine large wooden (later encased in corrugated iron) corn watermill, it was built at the turn of the nineteenth century on the River Ant in the Worstead hamlet of Bridge Gate. The first miller was John Balls. After two disastrous fires at the end of the nineteenth century it was reconstructed as a provender mill, and run in tandem with Ebridge Mill by Cubitt & Walker. Only part of the shell of this building is left today, after another fire in the 1970s.

Four

EAST RUSTON, SLOLEY, WORSTEAD, DILHAM AND SMALLBURGH

Pigeon shooting party in front of Worstead New Inn, c. 1910. This picture includes both the author's great-grandfather, Edward James Storey, and great-great-grandfather, William 'Billy Crackshot' Storey, seen on the left holding the release ropes for the baskets holding the pigeons. He did not shoot as his aim was 'too good' so he and Absolon Pattle acted as referees. The guns were only allowed to fire when the pigeons were level with the top of St Mary's tower.

St Mary's Church, East Ruston, *c.* 1910. This is probably little changed since Richard Porson, the son of the parish clerk, was born here on Christmas Day 1759. He demonstrated an astonishing memory, and local gentry and friends subscribed to his education through Eton. Entering Trinity College, Cambridge, he became in turn scholar, fellow and in 1792 Regius Professor of Greek.

East Ruston post office, *c.* 1910. For almost all its existence it was kept by Miss Anna Elizabeth Youngman, sub-postmistress.

Blacksmith's shop, Stalham Road, East Ruston, *c.* 1925. Left to right: George Barnes, carpenter, Billy Walpole, apprentice, Arthur James Plummer, who had followed in his father and grandfather's profession as the East Ruston blacksmith.

St Bartholomew's Church, Sloley, *c.* 1905. This parish of about 249 souls really did its bit during the First World War. The Revd Conrad Bankes BA served as an Army chaplain, but constantly wrote home, and his letters of hope were published in the parish magazine. Parishioners made over 208 bags of 'treasures' (chocolate cake, sweets and cigarettes) for Lady Smith Dorrien's Hospital Bag Fund. Ten men from Sloley were killed during the First World War, and are remembered on a fine stone cross erected in the churchyard.

Servants from Sloley Hall, *c.* 1895. At this time it was the seat of James Sewell Neville, lord of the manor.

Worstead station, *c.* 1910. Track right tablets are exchanged between the train driver and signalman, watched by Frederick Avery, the stationmaster. The station was built with finance from The Great Eastern Railway; the first stretch of rail from Norwich to North Walsham opened in 1874.

Station Road, Worstead, *c.* 1905. Henry Forder had his blacksmith's shop on the left. Nearby is Ammunition House Close, named after the brick building that stood here until 1814; originally it was the arsenal for the Tunstead Hundred and held 400lb of gunpowder in its vault. On the right of the photograph is Church Field, which Charles Themylthorp left as security for a weekly dole of bread to twenty poor locals.

Troops of the 1/6th (Territorial) Cyclist Battalion of the Norfolk Regiment throng Church Plain, Worstead, in front of the Manor House, 1916. A cycle school was established in the village for new recruits, such men being easily identified by their khaki shorts and grazed knees!

St Mary's Church, Worstead, 1900. The logs to be used in the restoration of the church roof fill the top of Church Field, observed by the rector, the Revd Thomas Jenkins. At the top of the church tower, 109 ft up, are the pinnacles that were added in 1861, but removed in the 1960s because of lightning damage. During the 1920s four boys scaled the old ladder in the church; standing on each other's backs they scrabbled on to the roof. Not to be outdone, one of the boys, 'Rock' Hannant, scaled a pinnacle, and, placing his stomach on the point, spread his arms and legs out like a star!

The architect consults his plans as the craftsmen work the logs for the roof renovations in St Mary's Church, 1900. They are working on great benches hauled on to the scaffold and supported high in the church roof. All works were completed for the grand sum of £1,100.

Church Plain, Worstead, *c.* 1910. A market was held here every Saturday until, as a result of plague, it was moved to North Walsham in 1666. An annual cattle and horse fair was also held on the Fairstead on 12 May, until the school was opened in 1845.

Honing Row, Worstead. Home to many of the author's ancestors, this was once nicknamed 'Storey Row'. Jimmy Davison, 'King of the Mole Catchers', is remembered working in the fields opposite. His prey, he told children, was tiny princesses in fur coats. Also living down here was Freddie Frosdick, who you could almost set your watch by as he passed the window on his way to garden for Lt.-Col. Walter Besant at Holly Grove House.

Worstead post office, The Round House, *c.* 1922. Postmaster at this time was James Copping. At about 8.50 a.m. almost every morning could be seen Austin Davison, the overseer, consulting his pocket watch as he awaited his driver, Narge Palgrave, to arrive to take him to the station. If Mr Davison was late the train would wait for him!

Christmas Henry Watts, Master Tailor, who retired in 1924, pictured in front of his shop, Back Street, Worstead. Another major trade of the village is indicated by the tall windows that maximized light and working time in weavers' cottages. There was once a time when almost every house in Worstead had a loom in it. These weavers brought in a good wage each week; by 1830 the weekly wage was 20–25s. This business was the flourishing life-blood of the village for over 500 years. The last weaver, John Cubitt, died in 1882 aged ninety-one. Behind these houses on the left stood St Andrew's Church, destroyed at the time of the Reformation.

Church and New Inn, Front Street, Worstead, 1900. Just in front of the church is the New Inn, built by Sir George Berney Brograve in 1825. This inn replaced the brewery standing next to the church at the request of the churchwardens, because drunken revellers seriously disturbed the Sunday service. Apparently the weavers sent their cloth to Norwich on a Saturday, and the agent returned the following morning to share out the proceeds.

Fishing party in front of The King's Head, Worstead, *c.* 1921.

Worstead Grange, House Hill, *c.* 1910. This was home to the Revd Frederick Walter during the 1920s and '30s.

Baptist chapel, Meeting House Hill, *c.* 1910. The original Meeting House was built in 1730 for fifty Particular Baptists, a group that was formed in 1717 under the leadership of Richard Culley. This chapel was replaced in 1829 by the one pictured. A stable for forty horses was also built at the same time for the many worshippers who travelled long distances. Six almshouses were built nearby in 1820 by Samuel Chapman, on land purchased from William Postle for £5.

St Nicholas' Church, Dilham, *c.* 1908. Four or five churches have stood on this site. The first recorded was built by William de Glanville in about 1125. The second, an impressive structure with tower, was built in about 1370 by Sir Roger Gyney. Falling into disrepair, it was completely demolished by 1835, including Sir Roger's armoured effigy lying beside his wife's, her feet resting on two dogs, and their entire tomb. The church illustrated here was demolished in 1930, and another church was built by Cornish and Gaymer in 1931. All that is left of Sir Roger's magnificent building is the font, which is still in use today.

Arthur John Page's butcher's shop, Dilham, 1922. This was opened before the turn of the century by Arthur's father, John, a smallholder from Dilham, in the old store beside their family home. The Pages served generations of villagers.

Dilham Football Club, *c.* 1920. The club is distinguished in that it has played on the same home field for over seventy years. The field itself was donated by Samuel Everett of Manor Farm after the First World War. As The Cross Keys was opposite it was used as their club house.

Dilham National School children, photographed as a souvenir of King George V's Silver Jubilee, 1935. The school was erected in 1876.

Dilham Water Mill, *c.* 1904. It was constructed at the turn of the nineteenth century along with a private staithe on the navigable waterway. Owned by Israel Lewis, at the county sessions in 1825 a jury assessed Mr Lewis entitled to £1,500 damages owing to the building of the North Walsham and Dilham Canal. The mill was working till the early 1900s and closed about 1910. Its last miller, Sidney Stackwood, went to Bacton Wood Mill, and Dilham Mills' machinery went to the First World War war effort. A few footings is all that remains of the mill today.

Low Street, Smallburgh, *c.* 1904. A group of farm labourers' cottages sprung up here after the enclosure of Smallburgh Common in the early nineteenth century. The street used to run from Norwich Road via the parsonage to Smallburgh Hill.

Smallburgh Hill, *c.* 1904. On the right is the post office, run at this time by Walter Marler Steadman, and also stocking groceries and drapery. Down the hill is The Crown, the first and still extant village pub, outliving the Union Tavern round the corner, which was kept during the 1920s by George Empson.

Smallburgh Post Office, c. 1930. The windows are crammed with everything from bottles of ginger beer and lemonade to biscuits, seeds, soap and underwear! The picture was taken a short while before the widow of Walter Steadman passed on, when the business was sold to George Read, who extended it to include carpentry.

Opposite the post office was Smallburgh Hill blacksmith's shop, which was kept by George Empson, who also farmed a smallholding. During the 1920s, and owing to changes in transport, the blacksmith's shop was taken over by John Bristow, a cycle agent. Shortly afterwards he diversified yet further to become a plumber, house decorator and founder of the filling station, still there today.

St Peter's Church, Smallburgh, *c.* 1910. The original tower fell in 1677. In 1885 the dilapidated chancel was restored by H.J. Green, a Norwich architect, and in 1902 the nave was restored to its original length, the roof renewed and a new bellcote erected for two bells. A tradition recorded that 'The Lord of the Manor of Smallburgh Catts cum Trusbutts gives annually on Lammas Day twenty-four eels to six pensioners of Smallburgh.'

Thimble Hill, Smallburgh, *c.* 1905. This stretch of the Norwich to Stalham road near Smallburgh has been travelled for hundreds of years, and has seen its turbulent times – especially during the 1450s when French raiding parties came up the Ant. Fears were such that farmhouses in the area were fortified, for example Dilham 'Castle', erected by Sir Henry Inglose.

Wayford Bridge Windmill, Smallburgh, 1906. This drainage mill a short way up Dilham Dyke had a slender brick tower of four floors, about 30 ft high. The mill was built by Englands of Ludham.

Wayford Bridge, Smallburgh, *c.* 1910. It carries the Norwich to Stalham Road over the River Ant, as it has done since time immemorial. Its predecessor was here when the River Ant was known as the Smale, and the Romans built a small outpost on the estuary to resist maritime assailants. In 1588 it was considered a strategic defence point by Captain York in his planned eastern defences against the Spanish Armada. In more peaceful times the North Walsham and Dilham Canal, which opened in 1826, started here. Today only pleasure craft ply its length.

This picture of Wayford Bridge, the ancient 'gateway' to the area we have explored, is a fitting conclusion to our journey around North Walsham and its surrounding villages.

Charles Mace's photographer's shop, Church Plain, *c.* 1960.

Acknowledgements

I should like to express my sincere gratitude to the following, without whose generous contribution of photographs, knowledge and time this book would not have been possible:

Brian Harmer • John Roper • Eric Reading • Michael Ling • Ivor Self
Frederick Mace AMPS • Dick Waters • Les Garnett • Simon Gorton
Stanley Lowe • Norwich Central Library (Local Studies Dept)
Norfolk Rural Life Museum • Eastern Counties Newspapers
Terry Burchell for photographic wonders, and Karen Powley
for typing a horrible scrawl into a book.

Very special thanks to my family, especially the elders, who have answered what must have seemed a multitude of questions, for their endless support and encouragement of this temperamental author.

Finally, but by no means least, thanks to the many people too numerous to mention who over the years have shared their memories, donated, inspired and helped me in my collecting and research.

If you enjoyed this book, you may also be interested in...

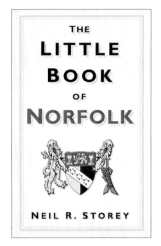

The Little Book of Norfolk

NEIL R. STOREY

The Little Book of Norfolk is a repository of intriguing, fascinating, obscure, strange and entertaining facts and trivia about one of England's most colourful counties. Armed with this fascinating tome the reader will have such knowledge of the county, its landscape, people, places, pleasures and pursuits that they will never be short of some frivolous fact to enhance conversation or quiz! A reference book and a quirky guide, this can be dipped in to time and time again to reveal something new about the heritage, the secrets and the enduring fascination of the county. A remarkably engaging little book, this is essential reading for visitors and locals alike.

978 0 7524 6160 1

Norfolk Folk Tales

HUGH LUPTON

The collective imagination of countless generations has populated the county of Norfolk with ghosts, saints, witches, pharisees, giants and supernatural beasts. Stories have evolved around historical characters, with Horatio Nelson, Oliver Cromwell, Anne Boleyn, Tom Paine and King Edmund becoming larger than life in folk-memory. This book is a celebration of the deep connection between a place and its people. For thirty years Hugh Lupton has been a central figure in the British storytelling revival. He tells myths, legends and folk-tales from many cultures, but his particular passion is for the hidden layers of the English landscape and the stories and ballads that give voice to them.

978 0 7524 7942 2

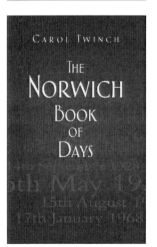

The Norwich Book of Days

CAROL TWINCH

Discover the rich and colourful history of Norwich with this collection of tales from across the city. Featuring a story for every day of the year, it includes tales of skirmishes, rebellions and battles as well as milestones along history's fascinating trail of popular culture. Why did Sir Thomas Erpingham build his famous gates at Norwich Cathedral? What connection does the war heroine Edith Cavell have with Norwich? And which ghost was said to haunt the city in the nineteenth century? Featuring events from shortly after its foundation right up to the present day, this fascinating selection is sure to appeal to everyone interested in the history of one of Britain's oldest cities.

978 0 7524 6589 0

Visit our website and discover thousands of other History Press books.

www.thehistorypress.co.uk